001.94
Aas

AASENG

The Bermuda Triangle

DATE DUE

SEP 2 9 2003			
NOV 0 8 2004			
NOV 1 8 2004			
SEP 2 7 2012			

The Bermuda Triangle

New and future titles in the series include:

Alien Abductions

Angels

The Bermuda Triangle

The Curse of King Tut

ESP

Extinction of the Dinosaurs

Haunted Houses

UFOs

Vampires

Witches

The Mystery Library

The Bermuda Triangle

Nathan Aaseng

Lucent Books, Inc.
P.O. Box 289011, San Diego, California

On cover: U. S. steamer *Yantic* in a cyclone

Library of Congress Cataloging-in-Publication Data

Aaseng, Nathan.
    The Bermuda Triangle / by Nathan Aaseng.
        p. cm. — (The mystery library)
    Includes bibliographical references.
    ISBN 1-56006-769-1 (hardback)
    1. Bermuda Triangle—Juvenile literature. [1. Bermuda
Triangle.] I. Title. II Mystery library (Lucent Books)
    G558 .A23 2001
    001.94—dc21

                                        00-011222

Printed in the U.S.A.

Contents

Foreword

In Shakespeare's immortal play, *Hamlet*, the young Danish aristocrat Horatio has clearly been astonished and disconcerted by his encounter with a ghost-like apparition on the castle battlements. "There are more things in heaven and earth," his friend Hamlet assures him, "than are dreamt of in your philosophy."

Many people today would readily agree with Hamlet that the world and the vast universe surrounding it are teeming with wonders and oddities that remain largely outside the realm of present human knowledge or understanding. How did the universe begin? What caused the dinosaurs to become extinct? Was the lost continent of Atlantis a real place or merely legendary? Does a monstrous creature lurk beneath the surface of Scotland's Loch Ness? These are only a few of the intriguing questions that remain unanswered, despite the many great strides made by science in recent centuries.

Lucent Books' Mystery Library series is dedicated to exploring these and other perplexing, sometimes bizarre, and often disturbing or frightening wonders. Each volume in the series presents the best-known tales, incidents, and evidence surrounding the topic in question. Also included are the opinions and theories of scientists and other experts who have attempted to unravel and solve the ongoing mystery. And supplementing this information is a fulsome list of sources for further reading, providing the reader with the means to pursue the topic further.

The Mystery Library will satisfy every young reader's fascination for the unexplained. As one of history's greatest scientists, physicist Albert Einstein, put it:

> The most beautiful thing we can experience is the mysterious. It is the source of all true art and science. He to whom this emotion is a stranger, who can no longer wonder and stand rapt in awe, is as good as dead: his eyes are closed.

Mysterious Terror

In the early morning hours of December 28, 1948, a DC-3 passenger airplane droned through the darkness over the Caribbean Sea. The flight from San Juan, Puerto Rico, to Miami had been a routine one for Captain Robert Linquist, a veteran pilot, and his crew. The weather was calm and they had experienced no mechanical problems.

At 4:13 A.M., Linquist radioed his position to flight controllers as he began his approach to the Miami airport. The DC-3 was fifty miles south of Miami, close enough for the captain to report, "We can see the lights of Miami now."[1] The thirty-six sleepy passengers, most of them New Yorkers who had been visiting their native Puerto Rico for the Christmas holidays, had nearly finished the first leg of their return trip.

The flight never made it to Miami, however. While on its final approach to the field, within sight of its destination, it suddenly vanished. Public safety officials launched a massive search for the missing plane. But despite the fact that the water in the vicinity of the plane's last known location was so shallow that a plane lying on the seabed would be easily visible from the air, officials never found a trace of the DC-3 or its passengers.

What could have caused the eerie disappearance of a perfectly functioning aircraft piloted by an experienced crew in excellent flying weather so close to its destination?

In the absence of any logical explanation, it appeared that the dreaded Bermuda Triangle had taken another victim.

Devil's Triangle

The story of the DC-3 was just one in a long line of unexplained disappearances cited by writers documenting the Bermuda Triangle mystery. The Bermuda Triangle is an area contained by a rough triangle that runs from southern Florida southeast through the Bahamas to Puerto Rico, then north to Bermuda and southwest back to Florida. More than one hundred airplanes and ships have apparently dematerialized in this 140,000-square-mile section of the Atlantic Ocean in the past half century alone, carrying over one thousand people to an unknown fate.

According to a stable of popular writers who alerted the public to the danger, not a single survivor or even a body

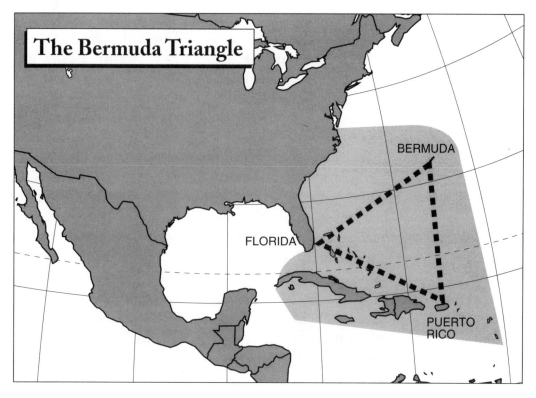

The Bermuda Triangle

has been found in any of these disasters. They claim no lifeboat, life jacket, or piece of wreckage from any of the missing craft has ever been left behind. The disappearances generally have taken place in clear weather during the winter months, often very near to shore, an airport, or land base. The airplanes and ships have been under the command of capable, experienced pilots and captains. In each case, disaster struck so suddenly that they were able to give little or no warning on their radios, and not a hint as to what danger they were facing.

Most curious of all was the fact that hundreds of airplanes flew through this same area of peril every day without running into anything that might account for the danger. Boats of all sizes churned through the waters of the Bermuda Triangle at all hours without incident. No one could predict when or where the deadly curse of the Bermuda Triangle would strike next.

The mysterious terror that lurks in the Bermuda Triangle has earned the area a host of grim nicknames. Some call it the Devil's Triangle, the Triangle of Death, the Hoodoo Sea, the Graveyard of the Atlantic, and the Limbo of the Lost. Although the official position of the U.S. Coast Guard and military authorities has been to deny that there is anything extraordinary about the Bermuda Triangle, unnamed authorities have been quoted as telling a different tale when speaking off the record. According to best-selling author Charles Berlitz, "Privately, both marine and aviation experts have confessed that they may be facing a phenomenon of the environment rather than a chain of technical mishaps."[2]

Several writers on the subject quote a U.S. Navy information officer as saying, "Nobody in the Navy sneers at this sort of thing. We've always known there's something strange about the Bermuda Triangle . . . It's almost as if these ships had been suddenly covered by some sort of electronic camouflage net."[3] Investigators have uncovered the fact that the Navy has been quietly conducting tests in the Bermuda Triangle under the code name Project Magnet as part of an effort to gain information about possible environmental disturbances.

Even the official inquiries into many of the Bermuda Triangle disappearances have expressed bewilderment as to what is going on. "Despite efforts by the U.S. Air Force, Navy, and Coast Guard, no reasonable explanation . . . has been made for the vanishments,"[4] declared a spokesman for the National Oceanic and Atmospheric Administration.

Intrigued by this haunting mystery, many people have taken on the role of detective. The solutions they have proposed cover nearly every conceivable possibility—including a few that stretch credibility to its breaking point. Some have argued that the Bermuda Triangle disappearances can

Rare natural weather forces are among the phenomena cited as possible causes of the Bermuda Triangle disappearances.

be explained by rare natural weather forces such as tidal waves, water spouts, sea quakes, and freak seas. Others have claimed the area is home to strange natural phenomena, far different from conditions found anywhere else in the world, such as reverse gravitational fields, black holes, and magnetic or electrical disturbances that distort radios, radars, and compasses. Still other investigators argue that what is happening in the Bermuda Triangle is so bizarre that it can be explained only by mind-boggling solutions out of science fiction, such as time warps, sea monsters, UFOs collecting samples from earth, underwater signal devices guiding invaders, the influence of remnants of a vanished civilization, and even the occult.

Is the Bermuda Triangle one of the most amazing and unnerving mysteries of our time? If not, what could possibly explain such a flurry of strange disappearances in so small an area?

Chapter 1

Ancient Fears and Legends of the Mid-Atlantic

Ever since humans first climbed into a boat and pushed off from the safety of the shore into the waters of the Atlantic Ocean, they have had to deal with stories of deadly menaces lying in wait for them. Fear of the unknown, the disappearance of ships in furious storms, and the incomprehensible size of the ocean combined to create fearsome legends about this sea of doom. Ancient mariners spoke of sea monsters lurking in the depths, of ships being swallowed by a sea of darkness. Only the bravest sailors from western Europe and Africa dared wander out of sight of the coast.

Typical of the superstitions that surrounded the ocean was the legend of the *Flying Dutchman*. According to the story, the *Flying Dutchman* was a ship that was caught in a fearful storm on the seas. Defying the elements, the captain sailed on, cursing the storm so savagely that he offended the gods, who doomed the captain to sail alone in his ship forever. According to the legend, disaster quickly overtakes anyone who sees this ghost ship on the seas.

Columbus and the Bermuda Triangle

Although there is some evidence that others may have risked journeys far into the Atlantic before him, Christopher Columbus led the first documented voyage across the mid-Atlantic and into the region now known as the Bermuda Triangle. Columbus kept a detailed captain's log in which he describes two curious events—the first indications that something strange was going on in this area of the world.

The first took place on September 13, 1492, when Columbus observed that his ship's compass needle had shifted. Instead of pointing directly to the north star, it now pointed six degrees to the northwest. Columbus worried about the effect this information would have on his crew. They were already nervous about sailing into the unknown. How would they react to evidence that they had reached a place where the laws of nature no longer applied? Columbus tried to keep this discovery a secret, but his crew

Christopher Columbus discovered a six degree shift in his navigational compass while sailing within the Bermuda Triangle.

included veteran sailors who discovered the compass shift on their own. When confronted, Columbus explained the shift by saying that apparently a compass needle did not point to the north star as previously thought, but pointed to something else. This turned out to be an astute guess (as scientists learned much later) and it apparently satisfied his men enough to continue the journey.

The second event occurred at 10 P.M. on October 11, when Columbus reported seeing a "remarkable ball of fire"[5] on the western horizon. It looked something like a lighted candle, and the crew at first thought they must be approaching some inhabited land. They soon found that this was not the case. Whether the fireball was a meteor or some unexplained phenomenon, it did not appear to upset the crew, which went on to find land shortly afterward.

The Sea of Lost Ships

Ironically, the most frightening element of nature that Columbus and his crew encountered in the Atlantic was not howling winds, violent storms, and towering waves but just the opposite. They sailed into a large area of the middle Atlantic—about the size of the United States— that was deathly calm. This region, whose western boundaries overlap the Bermuda Triangle, was so filled with floating seaweed that Columbus's crew at first thought they must be near land or at least in very shallow water. But they found no land, and their soundings showed the water was deeper than they could measure.

They had sailed into what eventually became known as the Sargasso Sea, named after the type of seaweed that dominated the waters. Its stillness is due to the fact that the major ocean currents, the Gulf Stream, the North Atlantic Current, and the Equatorial Drift converge on it from different directions. These currents revolve around the Sargasso Sea in a clockwise direction, leaving it as calm as

the eye of a hurricane, with little current, wind, clouds, or rain. The area was so frightening to Columbus and his crew because their ability to travel depended entirely on winds and currents. The Sargasso Sea had very little of either, and sailors feared they would get stuck in it until they died of thirst or starvation.

Over the years, ships sailing through the stagnant Sargasso Sea encountered the debris from many ships. Sailors took this as evidence that these ships met their doom in this sea. They dreaded the area and their fears spawned legends and folktales. Sailors warned of sea monsters and of slimy tendrils growing up around ships, holding them prisoner forever. The air was so still, said the sailors, that the crew could not breathe it, and died of suffocation.

Much of this talk was undeniably the result of overactive imaginations, triggered by fear and ignorance. Marine experts note that the ocean currents carry many things, including seaweed and ship debris, into the Sargasso Sea. These get caught in the unmoving stillness of the sea and remain there virtually forever. Bermuda Triangle researchers, however, note that for centuries the Sargasso Sea has been known to sailors as the Sea of Lost Ships.

Isle of the Devils

Records and communication were often spotty in past centuries, and so little is known about disappearances in the Bermuda Triangle during those times. All that was handed down was an ominous reputation. According to author Adi-Kent Thomas Jeffrey, the Bermuda Triangle is a "zone of disaster that has plagued man since the earliest days of seafaring in the new world."[6] Some of the oldest navigational records of the area label Bermuda as the Isle of the Devils.

Ship parts and seaweed collect in the still waters of the Sargasso Sea.

The earliest documented victims of the Bermuda Triangle suffered their fate less than a decade after Columbus's discovery of the Americas. On July 4, 1502, twenty-seven Spanish caravels set sail for Europe, loaded with an incredible haul of treasure from the New World. Included in the cargo was a solid gold table weighing more than three thousand pounds. The ships had barely started their journey through the Bermuda Triangle when a storm came up. All twenty-seven caravels were destroyed. The wrecks of ten of them were eventually found, but seventeen disappeared without a trace.

Later that century, Sir George Somers led a group of English adventurers bound for the Virginia colonies in their ship, the *Venture*. According to a journal kept by the members, they observed brilliant lights dancing across the sea and sky somewhere in the Bermuda Triangle. Shortly thereafter, a fierce storm blew up. The *Venture* was destroyed and the expedition barely managed to scramble to safety in the Isle of the Devils. The group managed to save one of the longboats, and they sent it out with a small, well-provisioned crew under the leadership of a man named Ravens, with instructions to sail to Virginia and bring back a rescue ship.

Ravens and his crew never reached Virginia. No clues as to their fate were ever found.

Alerting the Public

According to a number of popular authors who studied the subject, the area of the Bermuda Triangle has had a long-standing reputation as a ship's graveyard. The public, however, was largely unaware of any problem until the middle of the twentieth century.

That changed when an Associated Press reporter named E. V. W. Jones was looking for a story to enliven what *Time* magazine described as "a slow news day."[7] Intrigued by a

In St. George, Bermuda, a statue of Sir George Somers stands as a monument to his daring voyage across the Atlantic.

story of a mysterious airplane disappearance off the coast of Florida, Jones searched the files for similar stories in the same area. Amazed at the number of unexplained incidents in which no survivors or trace of the planes or ships ever emerged, he compiled the reports into an article, which he filed on September 16, 1950. The mystery of the vanishing planes and ships caught the eyes of editors around the country who then printed the wire service story. Occasionally, reporters would do a little digging on their own and find another disappearance or two to add to the list of unexplained incidents.

The term Bermuda Triangle was a creation of writer Vincent Gaddis, who plotted the location of the mysterious incidents and determined that they lay within a relatively small area in the shape of a triangle. Gaddis used the name in an article he wrote for *Argosy* magazine in 1964, and again in his book *Invisible Horizons*, published the following year.

By giving the mystery an easily recognizable name that clearly defined its boundaries, Gaddis helped fuel the public's fascination. Within a decade the Bermuda Triangle had become one of the hottest topics of discussion in the media. By 1974, nine books had been published on the subject, selling millions of copies among them. Charles Berlitz, grandson of a respected founder of language schools, achieved the greatest success with his number-one best-seller entitled, simply, *The Bermuda Triangle*.

Television picked up on the media frenzy with specials, including one narrated by the haunting voice of veteran horror-film star Vincent Price, and one studio even made a motion picture on the subject. With such saturation by the media in the 1970s, hardly a person in the United States was unaware of the deadly riddle waiting to be solved in the Bermuda Triangle.

Chapter 2

Ships Lost in the Triangle

The earliest mysteries of the Bermuda Triangle all have to do with ships for the simple reason that, until the twentieth century, ships were the only means of transportation in the area. The documented history of the Bermuda Triangle, as compiled by modern investigators, begins with a French freighter known as the *Rosalie*. In 1840, this ship was discovered adrift in the Bermuda Triangle area. The *Rosalie* appeared to be in excellent condition with its sails set and cargo neatly stored. Yet there was no one aboard. The crew left no clue as to their fate, and no sign of them was ever found.

Mary Celeste—Ghost Ship

A similar, better-documented ghost ship story concerned the experience of Captain Moorhouse and his ship the *Dei Gratia*. On December 4, 1872, they came across the *Mary Celeste*, a 103-foot vessel bobbing off the Azores Islands, which lie several hundred miles off the coast of Portugal. The *Mary Celeste* had sailed from New York several weeks earlier under the command of Captain Briggs. They had been carrying a load of cargo, including seventeen hundred barrels of alcohol to Genoa, Italy.

The captain's wife and daughter had sailed with him, along with a crew of eight. As no sign of life could be seen

The Mary Celeste *was found near the Azores Islands, pictured.*

aboard the ship, Moorhouse ordered some of his crew to board it and investigate. They found plenty of food and water. The cargo was all accounted for, and there were even children's toys on the captain's bed. But no one was aboard.

The puzzled crew examined the captain's log and found the last entry to be November 24—eleven days previous. According to Briggs's reckoning, the *Mary Celeste* had been five hundred miles to the west at that time. But the captain left no indication as to what might have happened to them. There was speculation that pirates could have killed the ships' hands, but then why did they not take any of the personal belongings on board, some of which were valuable? Nothing appeared to be missing except for some navigational equipment. The *Dei Gratia* crew found no sign of a struggle.

Captain Moorhouse placed his first mate and two crew members aboard the *Mary Celeste* and ordered them to sail alongside his ship to port in Morocco, six hundred miles away. At that time, ships that brought in abandoned or stranded ships or cargoes were entitled to a salvage fee from the ships' owners. But the disappearance of the *Mary Celeste* crew was so bizarre that Moorhouse found himself on trial for piracy. He barely cleared his name and eventually collected a small salvage fee, but no one ever solved the riddle of what happened to the *Mary Celeste*.

The *Ellen Austin* and the Diabolical Trap?

For sheer supernatural terror, none of the Bermuda Triangle stories can top that credited to the crew of the U.S. ship *Ellen Austin*. While sailing in the mid-Atlantic in 1881, the *Ellen Austin* came upon an unidentified, abandoned schooner. As with the *Mary Celeste*, the schooner was in good sailing condition with no indication as to what had befallen the crew. Captain Baker of the *Ellen Austin* put a few men aboard it with the intention of sailing it to port to collect the salvage money.

A violent seasquall arose and the *Ellen Austin* and the schooner were unable to maintain contact. Two days later, the *Ellen Austin* sighted the schooner and closed in on it. To the crews' horror, they found the schooner was again empty, with no sign of what had happened to their crewmates. According to author Richard Winer, Captain Baker was still determined to collect his prize money and he somehow persuaded three more crew members to man the schooner. He assured them that he would do everything in his power to keep them from being separated. As an extra precaution, he made sure all three men were heavily armed and he left instructions that they were to fire three shots at the first sign of any trouble.

This time a heavy fog rolled in. Despite the fact that the schooner trailed the *Ellen Austin* by only ten ship lengths, Baker and his crew lost sight of it. Within fifteen minutes, they backtracked to the exact spot where the schooner was last seen only to find that it had vanished.

Neither the schooner nor the latest unfortunate crew members were ever seen again. There were whispers that the schooner was some kind of a supernatural lure that drew sailors to their deaths.

Cyclops: "Only God and the Sea Know"

A disaster on a far greater scale captured newspaper headlines near the end of World War I. On January 28, 1918, a huge U.S. Navy ore ship, the *Cyclops*, steamed out of Brazil on its way to Norfolk, Virginia. The nineteen thousand-ton, 542-foot ship carried 309 crew members and a load of manganese ore that was desperately needed by U.S. industry supplying the military during World War I. Only eight years old, the *Cyclops* was a sturdy ship, equipped with a state-of-the-art radio system.

After making a stop in Barbados, the *Cyclops* took off on the final leg of its journey on March 4. For some unknown reason, the ship suddenly took a turn to the south, the opposite direction of its destination, shortly after leaving Barbados. Then it vanished, never to be heard from again.

The Navy was utterly baffled. All weather reports from that area indicated that seas were calm. The *Cyclops* sent no message to anyone indicating that it was in difficulty. The Captain, George Worley, was a twenty-eight-year veteran with a spotless record of service. What could have happened?

Amateurs and experts weighed in with their opinions. Some thought that the shifting cargo may have destabilized the ship or even ripped out its bottom. Yet even in such a case, there should have been time for some of the crew to abandon ship, and, given the favorable weather, they should have survived long enough to be picked up by rescue craft. And how could such an enormous ship disappear without leaving the smallest piece of debris behind?

In the absence of facts, wild speculation took over. The *Literary Digest* seriously suggested that the *Cyclops* may have been the victim of a giant octopus. A more popular

explanation cast suspicion on Captain Worley. Could the German-born captain have betrayed the ship into the hands of his native country, which was at war with the United States? But Worley's record of service, the fact that he left his wife and children behind, and the absence of German war records indicating any such plot made betrayal extremely unlikely. German naval records obtained after the war also discounted the notion that German submarines or mines could have blown up the *Cyclops*. Neither were in the area.

President Woodrow Wilson expressed the bewilderment of the entire nation over the loss of the largest Navy vessel ever to vanish without a trace when he declared, "Only God and the Sea know what happened to that great ship."[8]

In 1918, the Cyclops, *a U.S. Navy ship with state-of-the-art equipment, disappeared without a trace. Some speculated that it was the victim of a giant octopus.*

Sulfur Queen: **Silent Doom**

In February of 1963, another large cargo ship, the *Sulfur Queen*, headed out toward the Bermuda Triangle. The 425-foot ship left the port of Beaumont, Texas, bound for Norfolk, Virginia, with a crew of thirty-nine and over fifteen thousand tons of molten sulfur.

Early in the morning of February 2, the ship radioed its position as being 270 miles west of Key West, Florida. It was the last message ever heard from the *Sulfur Queen*. Search-and-rescue ships and planes crisscrossed the ship's projected route. This time they did not come up completely empty. A couple of life jackets from the *Sulfur Queen* were picked up a short distance from the ship's last stated position.

The Navy Board of Investigation conducted a thorough inquiry and came up with some possible causes of the disaster. One explanation was that there could have been an explosion in the cargo tanks where the sulfur had to be kept at 275 degrees to keep it in a liquid state. But industry

The Sulfur Queen, *a U.S. Navy cargo ship, disappeared in the Bermuda Triangle leaving behind two life jackets as clues.*

experts argued liquid sulfur was not a particularly hazardous cargo. Another possible cause may have been the weather. Some boats in the vicinity of the disappearance testified that high winds had created rough seas. Structural problems with the ship may have caused it to break in two or capsize under stress. Another possible explanation for the disaster was that in redesigning the ship to carry sulfur, engineers had to remove some of the bulkheads. These are the walls that separate the bottom of a ship into watertight compartments so that a leak in one section of the ship is contained. Without these bulkheads, any hole beneath the waterline could have caused the ship to sink rapidly. Alternatively, there could have been a steam explosion. The ship had experienced numerous fires in recent months. Perhaps one of these flamed out of control.

There was, however, no evidence to support any of these theories. Furthermore, in any of these cases, the *Sulfur Queen* should have left some wreckage. It should have at least had time to send out a radio message of distress. Why had it gone silently to its doom?

Witchcraft: Offshore Vanishment

Perhaps the most sudden disappearance involved a small boat appropriately named the *Witchcraft*. On December 22, 1967, Dan Borack invited a friend to go with him on a short trip in the *Witchcraft* to view the Christmas lights of Miami Beach. They were cruising no more than a mile offshore when the *Witchcraft*'s propeller struck a submerged object, disabling the engine.

Borack had no choice but to call the Coast Guard for a tow back to shore. According to Charles Berlitz, Borack provided them with his exact location at a specified buoy number. A Coast Guard boat immediately set out to the rescue and reached the location within eighteen minutes of the call. It found nothing.

In just a matter of minutes, the *Witchcraft* had vanished. Despite being within a mile of shore, the boat might as well have been in the middle of the deepest ocean, for no trace of it was ever found.

Scorpion: Bermuda Triangle Meets the Atomic Age

Even nuclear-powered submarines have not been able to escape the Bermuda Triangle legend. In May of 1968, the U.S.S. *Scorpion* and its ninety-nine-man crew headed back to its base at Norfolk from a tour of duty in the Mediterranean Sea. The *Scorpion* radioed a routine message from 250 miles west of the Azores on May 21. It was the last message ever received from the sub. The *Scorpion* disappeared. Again, there was no warning, no clue as to what had happened.

Several months later an oceanographic research ship detected some debris 460 miles south of the Azores on the edge of the Sargasso Sea at a depth of about ten thousand feet. Experts determined it was the *Scorpion*.

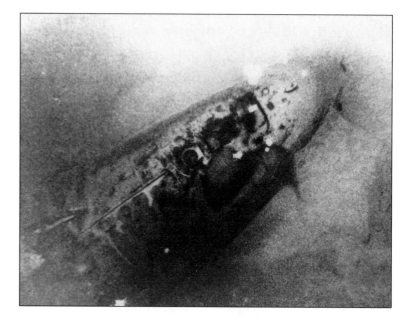

The remains of the U.S.S. Scorpion *were found at a depth of ten thousand feet and 460 miles south of the Azores.*

case incredibly bizarre, but it is thoroughly documented. Baffled radio operators heard the voices of the anguished victims describing their plight as they headed into oblivion.

At two o'clock in the afternoon of December 5, 1945, five officer pilots and nine crewmen took off on a routine practice run from Fort Lauderdale Naval Air Station, Florida. The mission of the TBM Avenger-torpedo bombers was twofold: first, they were to practice their torpedo bombing techniques on the abandoned wreck of a target ship stranded in shallow water just off the island of Bimini; then they were to run through an orientation exercise to see how well they could stay on course over open water. Their route was to take them 160 miles due east, then 40 miles north, and then west back to their Florida base. The entire flight was scheduled to last less than two hours.

Under the supervision of lead pilot Lieutenant Charles Taylor, a man with six years experience as a Navy pilot, the group completed their bombing assignment with no problems. The squad regrouped and headed out toward Great Stirrup Cay, in the heart of the Bermuda Triangle, in perfect flying weather—clear skies and a light wind.

This picture depicts a Navy TBM Avenger-torpedo bomber, such as those flown in Lieutenant Taylor's squadron.

At about 3:15, though, air controllers in Fort Lauderdale received an emergency message from Taylor. Somehow, the lieutenant, a man with over twenty-five hundred hours of flight time, had become disoriented. He did not know where he was or which way to go to return home.

When the base radio operators told him to head west, Taylor replied, "We don't know which way is west. Everything is wrong . . . strange. We can't be sure of any direction—even the ocean doesn't look as it should!"[9]

Radio communication between Flight 19 and the air station began to break up. Taylor was told to switch to a different frequency so they could stay in better contact. But he declined for fear that he would lose communications with the other planes in his flight if he did so. Unable to get through to Taylor, the Navy radio operators listened helplessly to radio communication between the planes complaining of compasses and gyros that had gone haywire.

At 4 P.M., Taylor suddenly handed over command of the squadron to Captain Stiver, a Marine pilot. From the garbled radio transmission, the authorities learned that Taylor thought they were over the Gulf of Mexico. Although there was disagreement about that among the group, the squadron was flying east in hopes of striking the Florida coast. In reality, they were over the Atlantic Ocean and their flight direction was taking them farther out to sea.

Mystery upon Mystery

Navy authorities responded to the emergency by dispatching a giant Martin Mariner rescue plane, manned by a crew of thirteen, after the Avengers. The Mariner sent a message to base reporting high winds above six thousand feet. It was the last message the plane would ever transmit. The plane and all thirteen crew members disappeared without a trace.

Meanwhile, disaster was closing in on the Avengers. They had fuel enough to fly for about six hours, or one thousand miles, which was a generous margin of safety for their scheduled two-hour run. But as they flew around in the Atlantic, trying to figure out where they were, their gas gauges steadily dropped.

Transmissions from Flight 19 eventually faded out, and so no one knows exactly where or how they met their end. A massive search involving more than three hundred aircraft and nearly three dozen ocean vessels was launched to find the missing men. Although the air search had to be suspended at dark, Coast Guard vessels searched through the night, and the air effort was resumed in the morning. Despite 930 air sorties that painstakingly covered 250,000 square miles of ocean over five days, the rescue team found nothing.

According to the popular Bermuda Triangle authors, the chain of events was all the more baffling because the crew of the Avengers were all experienced airmen. Author John Wallace Spencer noted that not only was Lieutenant Taylor a veteran flier but that the crew included men such as Sergeant Robert Gallivan, a Marine with four years of service, who had won medals for outstanding performance in battle in the South Pacific. What could these men have encountered that rendered all their training and experience useless?

Furthermore, even if the Avenger squadron had run out fuel and had to ditch into the ocean, they were equipped with rafts and other survival equipment. According to Spencer, "all crew were trained in ditching procedures and could exist for many days in the open sea."[10] Yet neither they nor any raft was ever located.

The unexplained loss of six aircraft and twenty-three men prompted one of the most thorough investigations in U.S. military history. The more officials looked into the matter, the more peculiar the incident turned out to be. At first, authorities believed the air station's instrument officer had to have been at fault for sending out planes with faulty compasses. But closer examination determined that all instruments had been checked out and were working properly before takeoff.

The mystery of the malfunctioning instruments grew more strange with the discovery that on the morning before Flight 19, another training flight had experienced an unexplained compass malfunction that had caused the pilots to land fifty miles north of their target.

Radio operators who had been monitoring the conversation between Taylor and the flight tower swore that, at one point, Taylor told a potential rescue pilot, "Don't come after me."[11] Why, they asked, would he say such a thing unless he was warning the rescue pilots of some overwhelming, perhaps even supernatural danger from which there was no escape? Had the Mariner rescue ship blundered into that deadly presence?

More eerie detail emerged. One of the five Avengers had been short one crewman. That person had been scheduled to fly with the group but at the last minute, for reasons he could not later explain, had changed his mind. Lieutenant Taylor had also requested, without explanation, to be relieved of duty for the flight. That request had been denied. Did both of these men sense some paranormal presence that warned them to stay away from the flight? There were reports of strange flashes and other unidentified flying objects in the sky over the eastern Florida coast that evening. Were these connected to the disappearances?

According to several Bermuda Triangle authors, Navy investigators could not make sense of the incident. Berlitz quotes Captain W. C. Wingard of the Naval Board of Inquiry as saying, "Members of the Board of Inquiry were not able to make even a good guess as to what happened."[12] Another member of that board marveled, "They vanished as completely as if they had flown to Mars."[13] Yet a third

Lieutenant Taylor was an experienced Navy pilot with more than 2,500 hours of flight time when his entire squadron vaninshed.

officer of the board summed up the investigation by saying, "This unprecedented peacetime loss seems to be a total mystery, the strangest ever investigated in the annals of naval aviation."[14]

Coincidence of the *Star* Sisters

More aviation mysteries followed closely on the heels of the Avengers loss. A large British luxury passenger airliner, the *Star Tiger*, stopped in the Azores in January 1948 before making the 1,960-mile flight across the Atlantic to Bermuda. On the night of January 29, it took off with twenty-five passengers and a crew of six, about an hour after another plane left the Azores on the same route. Although the aircraft encountered stronger than expected winds, the skies were clear and the first half of the flight went well.

At about 1 A.M. on January 30, the *Star Tiger* sent a message saying that all was going smoothly and gave its position as 440 miles northeast of Bermuda. Several hours passed, however, with no further communication from the airplane. Under normal safety rules, the long silence should have prompted radio operators monitoring the flight to check on the plane's status. Because they neglected to do so, no emergency was declared until attempts to contact the plane several hours later failed.

The *Star Tiger* was equipped with life rafts, each of which had a radio and a survival kit. But by the time rescue craft arrived on the scene, the weather had deteriorated badly. One rescue pilot commented, "I doubt anyone could survive in seas like that."[15] No sign of the missing aircraft was found.

An investigation uncovered the fact that the *Star Tiger* had a shaky maintenance record. Unexpectedly strong winds may have blown it slightly off course, and if it happened to miss sighting the island of Bermuda, it would have been in trouble as it did not carry enough fuel to allow it to reach any other airport.

But the disappearance was puzzling because, like the Avengers' Flight 19, the crew were experienced and well respected. Flying conditions were excellent and there was no SOS signal nor any indication of trouble from the *Star Tiger*. What really stunned some investigators, though, were the mysterious signals transmitted long after the disappearance. Operators reported hearing faint call letters, as if they were relayed from a great distance, nineteen hours after the last message from the plane. Those letters sound-ed as though they could have been those of the *Star Tiger*. Even more puzzling, a radio operator on February 3 picked up more faint signals in a crude code that spelled out s-t-a-r-t-i-g-e-r. Those familiar with the *Star Tiger*'s emergency radios said that the signal did not come from those radios.

"It may truly be said," concluded a court appointed by the British minister of civil aviation, "that no more baffling problem has ever been presented for investigation."[16]

But that was not the end of the matter. A year later, the *Star Tiger*'s sister aircraft, the *Star Ariel*, started off on a flight from London to Chile. The plane stopped at Bermuda to take on fuel. At 7:45 on the morning of January 17, 1949, the seven crew members and thirteen passengers took off for their final destination.

The *Star Ariel*'s fate was uncannily similar to that of its sister ship. Flying weather was excellent. At 8:40 A.M., the crew issued a report stating that all systems were fine. That was the last anyone heard from it. Inattentive operators were again responsible for a crucial delay before anyone realized the plane was missing. A massive search followed, with seventy-two aircraft covering 150,000 square miles of water. Not one piece of wreckage ever appeared.

Safety inspectors insisted there was no mechanical problem with the design of the two planes. Again, there had been no distress signals or any indication of a problem.

Stratotankers: Double Disappearance

Another multiple-plane vanishing act took place in the Bermuda Triangle on August 28, 1963. Two KC-135 Stratotankers left Homestead Air Force Base in Florida that day on a classified refueling mission over the Atlantic Ocean. These high-speed jets, whose main function is to refuel other aircraft in flight, were capable of flying at six hundred miles per hour and held nearly enough fuel to fly across the Atlantic to the Azores and back.

Debris thought to be from two KC-135 Stratotankers, was scattered so far apart that a mid-air collision seems unlikely.

At noon, one of the aircraft sent out a routine report from its position three hundred miles southwest of Bermuda and eight hundred miles northeast of Miami. As with the other incidents, both planes vanished without warning.

This time, however, rescue planes were able to locate debris at a site near the planes' last reported position. They collected three empty rafts and the flight helmet of Captain Gerald Gardner, one of the eleven crew members aboard the two planes. Since the two planes had disappeared at the same time, officials logically concluded that they must have somehow collided.

Two days later, however, searchers discovered more debris two hundred miles away from the first wreckage. Some Bermuda Triangle researchers suggested that this second debris pile was from the second plane. If that was true, it would disprove the theory that the planes had collided, for if they had, they would have hit the ocean very near to each other. The question was, if they did not collide, what could have caused both planes to crash in ideal weather without either being sufficiently alerted to the problem to call for help? Experts were hard-pressed to come up with any known environmental or mechanical problem that could explain it.

Outer Space Connection?

One disappearance happened to take place while astronauts were orbiting the earth in the vicinity. On June 25, a C-119, a bulky aircraft nicknamed a Flying Boxcar, vanished with its ten U.S. Air Force crew members over the Bermuda Triangle. As in other cases, there was no warning or signal of distress from the aircraft and no sign of it was ever found. Another plane flying at the same time in the opposite direction stated that the weather during the flight was absolutely calm.

This disappearance attracted particular attention because of what astronaut James McDivitt, peering out the window of his Gemini IV spaceflight, reported seeing at about the same time. McDivitt observed an unidentified flying object that was equipped with some sort of arm-like limbs, hovering over the Caribbean Sea. His observation was supported by his crewmate.

Adding to the mystery was the report by Charles Berlitz that, "As in the case of Flight 19, and other vanishing planes, faint and unintelligible messages were plucked up and soon faded out . . . as if the plane was receding farther and farther into space and time."[17] The incident of the Flying Boxcar fueled speculation that something or someone from another world was involved in the disappearances.

Repeating Pattern

The roster of unexplained aircraft disappearances over the Bermuda Triangle ran into the dozens. From 1945 to 1965, fifteen commercial airliners were lost in the area. Nine small planes vanished off the Florida coast in December 1949 alone!

Astronaut James McDivitt witnessed an unidentified flying object in the vicinity of the Flying Boxcar about the time of its disappearance.

Throughout the decades, the tragedies were remarkably similar. In July 1947 a U.S. Army C-54 flying a routine run from Bermuda never arrived at its destination, the Morrison Army Air Field at Palm Beach, Florida. The plane and its crew of six were last located forty miles off Bermuda. A British York transport carrying thirty-three passengers and crew across the Triangle to Jamaica vanished on February 2, 1952. In January 1967, three aircraft, carrying a total of eight passengers disappeared on short flights into the Bermuda Triangle. In each case, the weather was fine, the pilots were expert, safety-conscious fliers, no warning of danger was ever received, no trace of the planes was ever found, and the fate of the victims was never determined.

Chapter 4

Close Calls and Narrow Escapes

On September 10, 1971, an incident occurred that offered hope that some secrets of the Bermuda Triangle mystery might be revealed. Captain John Romero and Lieutenant Norman Northrup took off from Homestead Air Force Base that day in an Air Force Phantom jet. It was to be a short flight as the jet carried only seventy minutes worth of fuel. As four technicians tracked the jet on a radar scope, the blip showing the jet's location disappeared. Immediately, the controllers alerted rescue crews, who raced to the spot where the radar signal had stopped.

Within minutes, the search jets roared over the exact location of the disappearance. The odds were good that they would be able to find the jet and perhaps witness something that would explain the disappearance. But it was not to be. The Phantom was gone just like all the other planes, and the crewmen carried the secret of their tragic disappearance to the grave.

Incidents such as this convinced many that the Bermuda Triangle mysteries were so mystical and implausible, so foreign to all logical and scientific principles, that an

The island of Bermuda faces the northern corner of the Bermuda Triangle.

eyewitness account was the only way of determining what was happening. Unfortunately, none of the victims of the many incidents survived to tell what they knew.

There were, however, cases of people traveling on boats and planes in the Bermuda Triangle who reported weird experiences. Many Bermuda Triangle researchers wondered if the strange forces that these people encountered were the same ones responsible for the curse of the Bermuda Triangle. If these people were the fortunate survivors of the otherworldly force that plagued the area, their experiences could provide valuable clues as to what happened in these tragedies.

Close Calls in the Air

One of the first survivors of a strange encounter in the Bermuda Triangle was Dick Stein. In December 1944, Stein piloted one of a squadron of seven bombers flying from the eastern coast of the United States to the war front in Italy. His plane ran into such turbulence, on a clear day, that Stein barely kept his aircraft from being slammed into the water. Rather than risk going on, Stein left the squadron and returned to the United States. There he discovered that all six of the other bombers were reported lost.

No remains of them were ever found. Years later, Stein experienced an almost identical ferocious buffeting while piloting another plane over the same area.

Gerald Hawkes understood what Stein was talking about. Hawkes was a passenger on a commercial flight from New York City to Bermuda in 1952. Having just returned from duty in the Korean War, he looked forward to a period of rest and relaxation with friends. During the latter part of the flight, the four-engine aircraft suddenly plunged hundreds of feet straight down. While the frightened passengers were trying to collect their wits, the plane shot straight up into the air. In Hawkes's words, "It was as if a giant hand was holding the plane and jerking it up and down."[18]

Although the weather was clear, the pounding continued for nearly half an hour. When it was finally over, the captain announced that he was having trouble locating Bermuda, and that his radio was not working. Fortunately for the passengers, the captain was eventually able to get his bearings, or they, too, might have become victims of the Bermuda curse.

A member of a flight crew reported a different but equally frightening incident while traveling from San Juan, Puerto Rico, to New York in the 1960s. While flying at thirty-five thousand feet, the crew noticed streaks of static electricity forming on the windshield of the cockpit. As they watched in amazement, the streaks grew in number and intensity until the entire windshield glowed like a lightbulb. Shortly thereafter, the plane's gyros and compass, its two directional devices, gave conflicting readings. In an attempt to find out which was functioning correctly, the crew activated a battery-operated gyro kept as insurance in case the electricity went out. They were stunned when it gave a reading different from either of the other indicators.

The pilots somehow managed to reach safety, and when a mechanic examined the instruments he found that they had been zapped by a powerful electric shock, such as a bolt of lightning. Yet the crew insisted there had been no lightning; indeed, the skies had been clear and completely free of turbulence.

Perhaps the strangest report of a harrowing experience in the air came from Chuck Wakely. In November 1964, Wakely, an experienced pilot, was flying a charter plane for Sunline Aviation out of Miami. His assignment that late afternoon was to take a group of passengers to Nassau, Bahamas, and return to base.

Wakely began his return trip shortly after dark under clear skies. Before long, he observed a light far brighter than the normal twinkling of the stars. The glow turned out to be coming from his wings. It grew so brilliant that Wakely could hardly read the numbers on his instrument panel.

To his horror, his compass began spinning around and his electric autopilot stopped working. Wakely flicked on several switches and found that none of the electrical instruments was functioning properly.

By this time, the whole aircraft was aglow. With his instruments useless, Wakely gave up trying to steer and simply let the airplane fly on its own. Before he got into any serious trouble, the glow disappeared and all instruments returned to normal. Bermuda Triangle investigators could not help wondering if what he had experienced was the infamous force that had brought so many pilots and passengers to their deaths. Had he been one of the few lucky ones who had slipped out of the clutches of some killing phenomenon?

Ted Jones, a Miami construction worker who flew classic airplanes as a hobby, told of an experience as strange as any encountered in the Bermuda Triangle. Yet in his case, the weird phenomenon was not a spooky, alien force but an explainable natural occurrence. In the fall of 1969, Jones was piloting a short, solo flight from Bimini in the Bahamas to Miami. He expected the flight to last no more than forty-five minutes.

Shortly into the flight, he ran into a thick cloud bank. When he finally pulled clear of it, thirty minutes later, he expected to see the coastline of Florida. Incredibly, he found himself back where he had started, in the air over Bimini, still heading west! It was as if Jones had run into some sort of time warp that had blown him back a half hour into the past.

Jones's explanation was more scientific, if no less fascinating. He concluded that he had unexpectedly run straight into a 175-mile-per-hour head wind. For thirty minutes the gale had blown him backwards. While his plane registered a speed of 125 miles per hour, he was actually being pushed back at the rate of 50 miles per hour. Jones happened to be blown back to a location that he recognized. But it was easy to imagine a pilot becoming completely disoriented upon suddenly winding up one hundred miles away from where he or she expected to be.

Narrow Escapes on the Water

Those who sailed on the surface of the ocean in the Bermuda Triangle reported narrow escapes of a different nature. Don Henry sailed into a bizarre and terrifying stretch of chaos during a routine outing in 1966. The owner of a salvage business, Henry spent much of his time in the sea, hauling disabled or wrecked boats to shore. On this trip, he and twenty-three crew members were towing a heavy barge from Puerto Rico to Miami in their tugboat *Good News*.

Without warning, the boat's gyro began spinning in a clockwise direction. The magnetic compass also started

Numerous survivors of the Bermuda Triangle phenomenon say that their navigation and energy systems malfunctioned.

revolving like the second hand on a clock. Although there were clouds in the sky, the weather was not stormy, and Henry could see no reason for the disturbance. As he studied the sky and sea, everything went haywire. The horizon disappeared. The sky and sea blended until Henry could not tell where one ended and the other began.

He looked behind him and noticed the barge had disappeared. He had never even felt the snap of the cable. Despite the fact that he could detect no fog, the barge then reappeared moments later, tethered to the tug by its cable as if nothing had happened. Adding to the mystery, the *Good News* lost all communications. Its electrical generators continued to run but produced no energy. Fifty flashlight batteries that had been stored on board were completely drained. Although he arrived safely at his destination, a shaken Henry was totally at a loss to explain what had happened.

John Fairfax added a sensational element to the Bermuda Triangle mystery with his report of a strange occurrence in 1969. Fairfax spent half that year rowing a boat across the Atlantic Ocean from the Canary Islands to Fort Lauderdale. During a press conference to celebrate the completion of his quest, he told of seeing two flying saucers somewhere in the vicinity of the Bermuda Triangle. According to Fairfax, these greenish, glowing, disklike lights were ten times as bright as Venus. While watching them, he fell into a trance. "It was a funny feeling," explained Fairfax, "like someone was asking me to go away."[19] He felt as though he was risking grave danger to continue his voyage, although stuck in the middle of the ocean in a rowboat, he had no choice.

The most miraculous escape may have been that of Joe Talley in his fishing boat, the *Wild Goose*. Captain Talley had accepted a tow from the *Caicos Trader* on his way into an area of the Bermuda Triangle. Biding his time until his boat reached its destination, Talley fell asleep in his bunk. He awoke in terror to find seawater gushing in on him from all sides. Fighting desperately for his life, Talley worked himself free of the boat and found himself deep

On route to Fort Lauderdale, John Fairfax experienced a trance-like feeling in the Bermuda Triangle.

underwater. He kicked for the surface and after several agonizing seconds, in which he estimated he had climbed forty to fifty feet, Talley broke the surface.

Seamen from the *Caicos Trader* found him and pulled him out of the water. According to them, the *Wild Goose* had, without warning or reason, plunged straight down into the ocean as if sucked into a whirlpool. The shaken crew of the *Caicos Trader* had no choice but to cut the fishing boat loose or it would have pulled them under with it. Talley had been extremely lucky to escape before he, too, was dragged to the ocean bottom.

Norman Bean was another sailor who reported a freak phenomenon in the Bermuda Triangle area. In September of 1972, Bean had finished a fishing trip with three passengers in his boat, appropriately named the *Nightmare*, and was cruising back toward land in an area of the Triangle called Featherbed Banks. As he spotted the lights of his destination, he noticed something odd. According to his compass, those lights were in the wrong place. Had he not positively recognized his landmark, he would have followed a compass whose reading was suddenly a good ninety degrees off the mark.

When the lights on the *Nightmare* began to dim and then went out altogether, Bean grew eager to reach the safety of shore. Ignoring the compass reading, he steered toward the lights on shore. But after two hours of sailing, Bean found, to his horror, that he had gotten nowhere. The lights were as far away as ever. Meanwhile, Bean observed a large indistinguishable shadow in the sky that blotted out the stars on an otherwise clear night.

Not until the shape disappeared did the ship's compass and generator return to normal and the *Nightmare* was able to make shore.

The miraculous survival of a lone seaman in a major shipwreck shed light on what otherwise would have been another tragic Bermuda Triangle disappearance. On March 21, 1973, a 541-foot long Norwegian cargo ship, the *Norse Variant*, set out from Norfolk, Virginia, to Hamburg, Germany, with a load of coal from the Appalachian Mountains. Two days later, the huge ship vanished in a storm. Its last known position was 150 miles southeast of Cape May, New Jersey.

Rescue crews immediately set out to search for the ship and any survivors. Battling winds of eighty-five miles per hour and waves that swelled as high as forty-five feet, searchers covered 6,400 square miles. They found no sign of the *Norse Variant*. But to their amazement, on March 25, they discovered a lone man clinging to an orange raft that bobbed precariously amid the mountainous waves, some 300 miles east of the Virginia coast. Rescuers called it a one-in-a-million shot that anyone in a raft could have survived the storm long enough to be rescued.

The man turned out to be Stein Gabrielsen, a twenty-three-year old Norwegian seaman who had been on the

Sole Survivor of the Norse Variant, Stein Gabrielsen (left) was found floating on an orange raft days after a terrible storm sunk his ship.

Norse Variant. After two wild days of riding the stormy seas, he was exhausted but otherwise in excellent health. Gabrielsen explained that storm winds had ripped the cover off a 40-foot-square hatch. When the waves washed over the ship, they quickly flooded two cargo holds. Recognizing that the ship was doomed, the captain ordered the crew to abandon ship. Five minutes later, the *Norse Variant* was at the bottom of the ocean. Had Gabrielsen not been able to defy the odds, the tale never would have been told.

Eyewitness Confusion

Rather than helping to solve the mystery of the Bermuda Triangle, these accounts of the survivors and those who escaped their brushes with death only added to the mystery and confusion. Their descriptions of what they have encountered cover a wide range of possibilities ranging from stunning acts of nature like unexpectedly high head winds and giant whirlpools to eerie events far beyond the rational world. Taken as a whole, their accounts are as varied and as puzzling as the stories of the unexplained vanishings.

strange ship disappearances rivaled that of the Bermuda Triangle. According to several authors, at least nine ships vanished in this area between 1950 and 1954. All were large freight ships with good radio equipment. All vanished in calm weather, and only one of the nine was able to send out a distress signal. The Japanese government then sent a ship, the *Kaiyo Maru*, to investigate the area. After it, too, was destroyed—blown up by an underwater volcano—the Japanese government officially labeled it a danger zone.

The similarity between these two areas which shared the same unique magnetic circumstances led many to suspect something about their location seriously affected magnetism, causing a malfunction of instruments that resulted in disaster. Reports that the U.S. Navy spent years gathering information in the Bermuda Triangle as part of its Project Magnet lent further credibility to those who suggested that unusual magnetic behavior was responsible for the mid-Atlantic disasters. Charles Berlitz claimed that, despite their official denial of concern over the Bermuda Triangle, the U.S. Navy and Coast Guard both recognized that compass readings in the Bermuda Triangle were extremely variable.

There were, however, some glaring flaws in the Bermuda Triangle–Devil's Sea magnetic connection. The Navy said its studies found no abnormal magnetic disturbances in the area. Critics pointed out that the only logical effect of an area having no variation between the magnetic and true north poles is that it should reduce the chances for navigational error. After all, it eliminates the need for making a mathematical conversion from the compass reading to the correct directional bearing.

Furthermore, the Bermuda Triangle is a large area. While magnetic variation between the poles is zero near Florida, it is as much as fifteen degrees in other parts of the Triangle. This meant that if there were any strange effect from zero variation, it should not affect most of the mystery area.

Finally, critics noted that the Bermuda Triangle and the Devil's Sea are not unique in having no magnetic variation. All places on a longitudinal line that runs from the poles through Florida and around the world to the Devil's Sea also show no magnetic variation. All along that line, the two poles line up perfectly. This includes many places in the United States and Canada where no unusual magnetic phenomena have been detected.

Ronald Waddington, another Bermuda Triangle theorist, suggested that the vanishing could be a result of magnetic destruction caused by underwater volcanoes. According to Waddington, such volcanoes, which may be unusually active below the Bermuda Triangle, "are constantly shooting chunks of radioactive, densely magnetic matter into the air, short-circuiting the electrical equipment of passing planes and causing them to nose-dive into

One Bermuda Triangle theorist suggests that an underwater volcano emits radioactive material above the surface of the water causing disasterous effects to planes and ships.

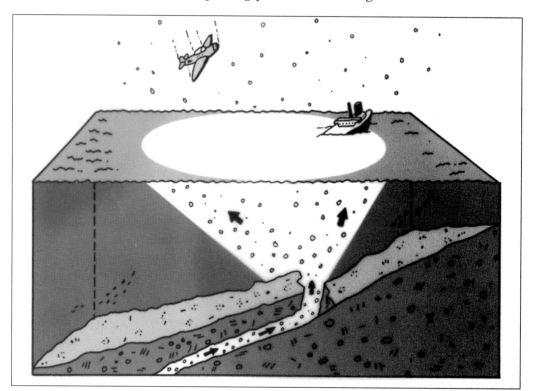

the ocean. As for ships, chunks of this radioactive material could shoot to the surface with the velocity of a hydrogen bomb and home in on the steel hulls of ships like the magnetic head of a torpedo."[20]

Scientists noted, however, that no research exists to support this theory.

Other Scientific Explanations

Curious about the fact that radio contact in most Bermuda Triangle disappearances was nonexistent, some theorists have suggested that the area may be filled with radio dead zones. There are, in fact, small areas within the Triangle as well as outside it where radio contact can be difficult. This theory, however, would explain only why communication between the victims and the outside world was cut off, not what caused the disasters.

Some Bermuda Triangle theorists stretched the known limits of science in their attempts to explain the disappearances. Author Ralph Baker offered the idea that antigravitational matter may exist within the Triangle. Similarly, some suggested that a void exists within certain areas of the Triangle in which the normal laws of gravity, magnetism, and electricity do not apply. Others speculated that black holes may be at work. Black holes are areas of such incredible density that anything that comes within their gravitational pull gets sucked into them. Nothing can escape—not light or radio waves—which would explain the absence of any trace of the vanished objects. However, while black holes have been discovered far in space, scientists considered the idea of their existence on earth extremely far-fetched.

Alien Invaders

Some of the most popular theories went well beyond traditional science. John Wallace Spencer, a Bermuda Triangle researcher who spent ten years in the U.S. Air Force, and M. K. Jessup, a science writer, were two of many who argued that the disappearances were caused by alien beings.

Spencer admitted that the idea of beings from another planet causing the Bermuda Triangle disappearances is hard to swallow. But, he explained, "Since a 575-foot vessel with 39 crew members disappearing 50 miles offshore in the Gulf of Mexico and commercial airlines disappearing while coming in for a landing cannot happen according to earthly standards and yet *are* happening, I am forced to conclude that they are actually being taken away from our planet for a variety of reasons."[21]

Alien abduction advocates pointed out that such disappearances appear to involve powers beyond human understanding. For example, if electromagnetic force fields or antigravity fields suddenly appear on earth, where no one has previously encountered them, it is reasonable to assume that they have been introduced by beings who know how to use them. This higher power would, logically, be a life form from a different solar system.

According to authors such as Berlitz, the number and intensity of UFO sightings were far greater in South Florida than in other areas of the world. Richard Winer, however, disagreed, saying that even UFO researchers admit there are dozens of areas where more UFOs are reported. Spencer then argued that the reason why more mysterious disappearances occurred in the Bermuda Triangle was not because of more UFOs in that spot but because large amount of traffic through fairly empty waters provided greater opportunities for aliens to make unobserved abductions. Still others believed that there were underwater signal devices within the Bermuda Triangle that guided the invaders to the target. In the absence of documented evidence, however, many people were reluctant to embrace such controversial and fantastic explanations.

The Lost City of Atlantis

Perhaps the most astounding theory of the Bermuda Triangle mystery was that it was the result of a vast underwater civilization. Such Bermuda Triangle researchers as Sanderson strongly promoted this idea and Berlitz devoted several chapters to it in his best-selling book.

The basis for the belief was an ancient legend about a mighty empire, known as Atlantis, that once existed on an enormous island in the Atlantic Ocean. Stories of its existence were widespread—even the ancient Greek philosopher Plato referred to it in his writings. According to the stories, Atlantis was a land of great wealth, and its people were far superior in intelligence to anyone of their day. At about 9500 B.C, the island was suddenly swallowed up by the ocean and disappeared without a trace.

The legend of the lost continent of Atlantis remained part of folklore for many centuries. The stories resurfaced in the mid-twentieth century because of the work of Edgar Cayce. From 1923 until his death in 1945, Cayce frequently

Some believe the legend of the lost continent of Atlantis is related to the strange occurrences within the Bermuda Triangle.

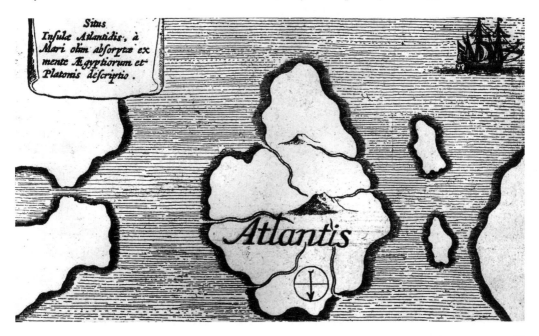

Situs Insulæ Atlantidis, à Mari olim absorptæ ex mente Ægyptiorum et Platonis descriptio.

Atlantis

went into what were described as psychic trances, during which he related extraordinary predictions and other information. He awoke remembering nothing of which he spoke during his more than twenty-five hundred trances.

Among his pronouncements were numerous declarations relating to Atlantis. Cayce spoke of Atlantis as being the size of Europe and Russia combined. The great civilization was powered by generators made of gigantic crystals that harnessed the power of the sun to their own uses. According to Cayce, the people of Atlantis may have brought on the catastrophe by misuse of their power crystals.

Among Cayce's more intriguing claims was that a new land, which many took to be Atlantis, would emerge off the coast of Miami in 1968 or 1969. It happened that in 1968, underwater explorers discovered massive stone ruins in thirty feet of water west of Bimini, just where Cayce had specified, fifty miles off the Florida coast.

To many who believe in psychic powers, this was evidence that Cayce's claim that Atlantis was real. From there, it was a small step to claiming that this lost city was related to the Bermuda Triangle. Some claimed the advanced Atlantean civilization was still in existence beneath the sea and that they periodically plucked samples of the primitive over-sea world. Others said that the ship and plane disappearances were unintentional and unpredictable by-products of the powerful energy crystals still in use on Atlantis.

Recognizing that the supposed existence of an under-sea community stretches credibility to the breaking point, some tried to blend the tales of Atlantis into scientific explanations. Charles Berlitz, in his 1977 book *Without a Trace*, put forth the notion that remnants of the immense power source that destroyed Atlantis could be responsible for the Bermuda Triangle disappearances today. Perhaps it was this concentrated energy source deep in the ocean that played havoc with compasses, electricity, and radios.

The famous psychic Edgar Cayce, declared that the civilization of Atlantis ended catastrophically by misuse of their crystal powers.

The idea that an ancient, underwater civilization might have solar power installations, lasers, or other death rays and that this technology might be responsible for the Bermuda Triangle disappearances intrigued many but raised more questions than it answered. Namely, how could such equipment—if it ever existed—be operable after thousands of years in the ocean?

Multiple Dimensions and Time Warps

Bermuda Triangle authors insisted that many scientific truths have been discovered over the ages only because scientists were able to break through the traditional boundaries of accepted thought. As a result, they offered for consideration theories that boggle the mind, such as multiple dimensions and time warps.

Sanderson and others suggested that there could be a parallel world in another dimension that occupies the same time and space as our world. Perhaps there are doors or windows that occasionally open up for brief periods between our world and that world. Perhaps objects sometimes drop out of one world into the other. It could be that the Bermuda Triangle contains such doors or windows and that the vanishing planes and ships have slipped into that other dimension. Perhaps they are still there.

Intrigued by the indications that confusion about time is as common an element of Bermuda Triangle disappearances as confusion about location, some proposed that pilots have been caught in a time warp—a small area in which time does not pass normally. Time warp would explain the mystery of the faint message that was heard some five days after the *Star Tiger*'s destruction. One author suggested the survivor was caught in a warp where time moved super quickly. He arrived at February 3 in a few moments, so that when he tapped out his message, he was five days ahead of the normal world in relation to time.

A different otherwordly slant came from Connecticut psychic Ed Snedeker, who claimed he was able to make contact with some of the victims of Bermuda Triangle disappearances. He explained that a number of funnels, invisible to the human eye, are dispersed throughout the world. These funnels lead to depositories located in hollow and remote parts of the earth wherein the victims are kept in a sort of time-space limbo. They are powerful enough to suck up people and objects as large as ocean freighters. "Although they are not visible and will never be seen on this Earth again, they are present and their voices can be heard,"[22] Snedeker said of the victims.

Unresolved Mystery

None of the theories about the Bermuda Triangle came close to laying the mystery to rest. The lack of a clear-cut explanation for the sudden disappearances, together with the widespread suspicion that something extraordinary was behind them, helped fuel public fascination with the subject. For several years in the early 1970s, the Bermuda Triangle ranked as one of the most terrifying and mind-boggling puzzles on Earth.

Chapter 6

The Rest of the Story

In 1975 a new book written by a librarian at Arizona State University cast the Bermuda Triangle mysteries in a whole new light. The book's author, Larry Kusche, spent hundreds of hours meticulously researching the bizarre happenings in the Bermuda Triangle. Kusche published his discoveries in a book called *The Bermuda Triangle Mystery: Solved*.

Unlike previous research efforts, Kusche's book did not seek to explain how the disappearances occurred. Instead, his book called into question the entire premise of the Bermuda Triangle. He found no evidence to support its existence but uncovered a great deal of misinformation fueling the centuries-old mystery.

Fact or Fiction

Kusche traced the origin of the *Ellen Austin* story to a brief account given by a man named Gould in a 1914 book. According to this version, the *Ellen Austin* found an abandoned ship in the mid-Atlantic in 1881 and put a few crew members on board to take it in to port. On their way to Newfoundland the ships became separated in a fog. When the *Ellen Austin* resighted the abandoned ship, they found their crewmates had vanished.

Kusche became suspicious when an article by Vincent Gaddis cited Gould as the source of his story, but changed many of the facts from Gould's version. Gaddis's account added the story of the second crew put on board and the tale of its disappearance. Other Bermuda Triangle authors embellished that story, adding a few more details here and there for interest.

Kusche then set out to do what none of the other authors had done—verify the accuracy of the story. He spent more than one hundred hours combing through newspapers from the *Ellen Austin*'s destination (either Newfoundland or Boston, depending on the source), around the time of the incident. Despite the front page sensation that such a story would have produced, not one paper reported it. He found it highly unlikely that such a story, had it actually occurred, would have gone unreported.

Kusche spent tedious hours studying shipping records and found no evidence that several ships that supposedly disappeared in the Bermuda Triangle ever existed. Norway, for example, has no record that a ship called the *Stavenger* was lost in 1931, as Bermuda Triangle authors claimed.

The Expanding Triangle

Kusche produced evidence that the boundaries of the Bermuda Triangle had been greatly stretched to accommodate many of the disappearances. Disasters chalked up to the Bermuda curse actually happened as far away as Ireland, Africa, and the Pacific Ocean. The *Mary Celeste* vanished far north of the Bermuda Triangle, as did the *Raifuki Maru*. The *Sulphur Queen* disappeared west of Florida; the *Scorpion* went down near the Azores, far to the east of Bermuda. In some cases, the missing ships passed through the Bermuda Triangle but could have disappeared anywhere along their route.

Even those who most strongly believed that a mysterious force caused the vanishing felt uncomfortable about the discrepancies. Gaddis admitted that he should not have used the term Bermuda Triangle to describe the area of disasters. Other authors, such as John Wallace Spencer, adjusted the boundaries to include a far wider area of the ocean, called the Limbo of the Lost. Some included the Gulf of Mexico, some pushed the boundaries east all the way to the Azores. But even boundaries stretched to include a huge portion of the Atlantic could not explain how the German ship *Freya* became a part of the Bermuda Triangle roster. A supposed victim of the Triangle in 1902, the *Freya* actually went down off the west coast of Mexico.

The *Atalanta* may have gone down with its 300 crewmen in the Bermuda Triangle but chances are much better that it did not. No one knows where the ship vanished, but only 500 miles of its 7,000 mile journey crossed the Triangle.

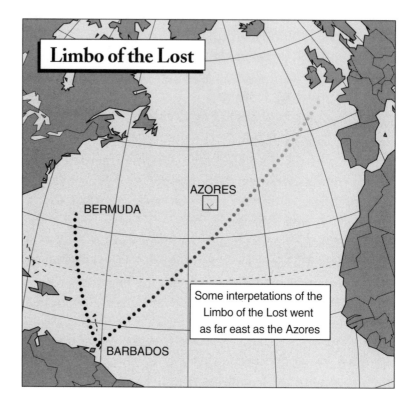

Limbo of the Lost

AZORES

BERMUDA

Some interpetations of the Limbo of the Lost went as far east as the Azores

BARBADOS

Sloppy Research

Kusche uncovered evidence that Bermuda Triangle advocates neglected to report all the facts of many disappearances. In the case of the *Rosalie*, the French ship mysteriously found abandoned on the seas near Nassau, Bahamas, in 1840, Kusche found no record that any such ship ever existed. In searching the records of Lloyd's of London, a ship-insuring company, he did find documentation of a ship called the *Rossini*, found abandoned near Nassau in 1840. But according to the company's records, the ship ran aground and all crew and passengers were saved. Those who found the ship later apparently were simply unaware that all hands had been rescued.

The 1963 case of the two KC-135 Stratotankers proved to be a case of extremely sloppy reporting. Bermuda Triangle authors cited a news report that a second patch of debris was sighted nearly two hundred miles away from the first, proving the planes could not have collided but had mysteriously gone down at the same time. The *Miami Herald*'s report of the event, however, clearly stated, "Another patch of debris was sighted Friday about 160 miles away, but searchers said Saturday that none of it came from either of the two planes."[23] In fact, it turned out to be nothing but a buoy caught in a mat of seaweed and driftwood. The Air Force saw no reason to alter its conclusion that the planes had collided.

Some of the easiest claims to verify or disprove were the reports that the ships and planes had disappeared in clear weather. Kusche contacted the National Climate Center, in Asheville, North Carolina, to obtain records about weather conditions during the mysterious disappearance of the *Cyclops* in 1918. He discovered that gale warnings had been issued for a wide area along the coast during its voyage. This fact had been overlooked because the Navy was only looking at the weather near the *Cyclops*'s last sighting south of that area.

Gale warnings issued along the course of the Cyclops *may explain its disappearence.*

A similar story occurred with the *Suduffco*, the freighter that sailed from Newark, New Jersey, in 1926. According to Bermuda Triangle authors, the ship and its crew mysteriously vanished without a trace. But by simply reviewing news reports from that time, Kusche learned that the *Suduffco* sailed into an incredible storm off the eastern coast of the United States. One captain who passed the *Suduffco*, sailing in the opposite direction, barely made it to New York. He described the seas as the worst he had ever seen.

The same circumstances surrounded the loss of the Cuban ship *Rubicon* in 1944. Weather records show that a hurricane slammed into the East Coast of the United States while the ship was in the vicinity. Given relevant weather information, the disappearance of the *Cyclops*, *Suduffco*, and *Rubicon* are not as mysterious as claimed.

There were even cases in which Bermuda Triangle advocates not only neglected to research their information but actually distorted the facts. A prime example of this distortion was the legend of the Devil's Sea near Japan. One of the coincidences cited by Bermuda Triangle advocates was the claim that this area, with a latitude and other features similar to that of the Bermuda Triangle, caused a similar rash of bizarre and unexplained disappearances.

Kusche found, however, that the "almost a dozen large ships"[24] that Bermuda Triangle authors reported as having mysteriously vanished in the area were actually small fishing boats that had been lost in bad weather. The *Kaiyo Maru*, the ship supposedly sent to investigate these strange disappearances, was actually sent on a research expedition to study underwater volcanic activity in the region before the other boats were lost.

The *Kaiyo Maru* was, in fact, destroyed by one of these volcanoes, and the Japanese authorities did warn sailors to beware of the area. The caution, however, was issued only because of the unpredictability of the volcanoes. Kusche found that, contrary to its supposed terrifying reputation, virtually no one in Japan had ever heard of this Devil's Sea.

What Happened to Flight 19?

The most important story that Kusche examined was the disappearance of Flight 19. For years it stood as the cornerstone of the Bermuda Triangle legend. As related by best-selling authors, it defied rational explanation. How could five experienced Navy Avenger pilots and the rescue team sent after them vanish without a trace in clear weather? What about the expressions of bewilderment uttered by authorities in its wake?

The events of that disappearance are, in fact, well documented, thanks to radio communications between the squadron and its base and to an extensive, four-hundred-page military report that followed. Kusche learned that while Lieutenant Taylor, the lead pilot, was experienced, the others were not. The other pilots and all but one of the crew were students in training.

While the weather was excellent at the start of the mission, it did not stay that way. One ship in the area reported high winds and enormous waves. The flight apparently ran into an unexpected eighty-mile-per-hour head wind midway into the flight. This, plus a malfunction of the lead pilot's compass, caused Taylor to temporarily lose his bearings. While he was an experienced pilot, Taylor was not familiar with the Bahamas.

Senior flight instructor Robert Cox received a message from Taylor that both his compasses were out and that he thought he been blown over the Florida Keys, to the southwest of Florida. Given that information, Cox suggested that Taylor fly with the sun on his port (left) wing—that would take him north up the coast. Cox was preparing to fly out to find the flight and guide them home when Taylor appeared to get his bearings. "I know where I am now," he said. "Don't come after me."[25] Rather than being a warning to the rescuers to stay away from whatever terror had engulfed him, this was simply an indication that, for a brief time, Taylor thought he was okay.

Taylor turned over the lead to another pilot because that pilot's plane had a working compass. The problem at this point was not that they did not know which direction was west, but that they did not know where they were. In reality, Flight 19 was very near where it was supposed to be—near the Bahamas, to the east of Florida. At some point in the late afternoon, radio controllers at Port Everglades, Florida, believed Taylor's estimate of his position was mistaken. But Taylor continued to believe he was over the Gulf of Mexico. Radioman Melvin Baker testified, "I think that I never convinced him that I knew what I was doing."[26]

Radio contact between the base and the flight began to break up. Taylor's refusal to switch to a different emergency frequency that would ensure clear communications proved fatal. At 5:20, the base lost two-way communication with Flight 19. They could pick up the flight's transmission but the static was so heavy that they could not get through to Taylor. About forty minutes later, flight monitors were able to confirm Flight 19's position out in the Atlantic, north of the Bahamas but were unable to get the information through to Taylor. Taylor continued to believe he had to fly east to reach base when that course was only taking him farther out to sea. At least two of the students appeared to disagree with him and wanted to fly west, but military discipline had taught them to stay together.

According to the Bermuda Triangle legend, the last transmission from Flight 19 came at 4:25 P.M. A Martin Mariner PBM flying boat, capable of staying in the air for twenty-four hours, then took off in clear weather to rescue the lost crew. It vanished without a trace.

In reality, Flight 19 continued transmitting until 7:04 P.M. as Taylor tried to figure out where he was. The Avengers had enough fuel to last until about 8:00 P.M., at which time they would have to ditch into the ocean. The Navy sent out not one but two Martin Mariner PBM flying boats shortly before 7:30, heading for Flight 19's last reported position. By this time, the weather had deteriorated badly. One of the Mariners failed to report its position as scheduled at 8:30. Witnesses boating off the coast testified

The disappearance of Flight 19 may be attributed to inexperience in the flying area, student flight crews, and bad weather.

that they saw a plane catch fire in the sky, plunge into the water and explode in the area where the Mariner was flying. Because of the amount of fuel they carried, Mariners were nicknamed flying gas tanks, and such an explosion was one of the hazards they faced.

Far from being baffled by unexplainable events, the Navy was quite certain of what had happened. The Martin Mariner had caught fire and exploded far from the area in which the Avengers were floundering. As for Flight 19, the pilots flew around, lost, until they ran out of fuel and had to ditch. By that time, a storm had come up. Search planes reported extreme turbulence, gale-force winds, and high seas. The men could not last long in such a perilous sea, and darkness had descended, making finding them nearly impossible.

Regarding the paranormal angle of crewmen requesting to skip the flight, the facts proved less than mysterious. Corporal Allan Kosner, the Marine who decided less than an hour before takeoff not to go on the flight, had completed his required flight time for the month. He had no reason to go and was excused.

The complete story of Flight 19 revealed a tragedy, bad luck, and perhaps questionable judgment, but no haunting mystery.

The Miami Mysteries

The DC-3 passenger flight from Puerto Rico to Miami in 1948 also recedes from the edge of the twilight zone as more facts are uncovered. An investigation showed that the plane had been experiencing problems with its communications and electrical systems. Its batteries were low when it took off from Puerto Rico, but the captain declined to recharge them since the process would take a long time and would put them far behind schedule.

Bermuda Triangle authors stated that the plane approached within sight of the Miami airport, and Berlitz

Corporal Allan Kosner had completed his required monthly flight time and was excused from Flight 19.

even quoted Captain Linquist as sighting the lights of Miami. That proved to be an assumption based on the belief that a plane within fifty miles of Miami would have been able to see the city. There is no documented evidence that Linquist ever saw Miami.

Contrary to the impression given by the authors, Linquist never made contact with the Miami control tower at all. His communication stating his position as fifty miles south of Miami was picked up, very faintly, by a New Orleans tracking station.

Kusche noted that this reported position was not necessarily accurate but was merely Linquist's estimate of where they were. For an hour and a half, the plane was not in contact with anyone, probably a continuation of the transmission problems it had previously experienced. A shift in the wind could easily have pushed the plane south of where Linquist supposed it was. Even if the plane had been on course, its route would have put it southeast of Miami, not directly south. At any rate, it is likely that the DC-3 went down nowhere near the easily searchable twenty-foot depths that Bermuda Triangle mystery buffs claimed.

Investigators, in fact, concluded that the flight probably flew off course to the south and missed Florida. Its malfunctioning navigational equipment would have left the captain with no way of knowing where he was or how to get to safety, and the failure of the communications system cut him off from any assistance. Most likely, the flight flew over the Gulf of Mexico, hoping to find land until it ran out of gas and fell into the sea.

The mystery of the *Witchcraft* boat that vanished within a mile of Miami while looking at Christmas lights proved to be another sad but understandable tragedy. The weather was too rough for such a small boat to be out, with whitecaps measured at over six feet. Having lost power, the boat's captain had no way of keeping his boat positioned properly against the waves. A six-foot wave catching the *Witchcraft* broadside would easily have capsized it.

The claim that the boat's captain, Dan Borack, issued his exact position at a numbered buoy to the Coast Guard is an invention. In reality, the Coast Guard asked Borack to give them twenty minutes to reach the area and then fire a flare to guide them to his location. They never saw the flare. When they arrived near the scene in the dark in a roiling sea, their chances of finding any remnant of the *Witchcraft* or its occupants were near zero.

A Relatively Peaceful Area?

Kusche and others also studied the statistics and concluded that they simply do not support that idea that the Bermuda

Triangle is a death trap for ships and planes. Kusche looked at the accident data that Ivan Sanderson had claimed as the basis for his belief in the existence of the accident-prone Vile Vortices. He noted that even Sanderson's shaky data actually found only a few of these supposed vortices and that from those he assumed the existence of the others. Other researchers who were more learned in the area of statistics said that the evidence did not support the existence of any Vile Vortex, including the Bermuda Triangle. In fact, Michael Shermer, author of *Why People Believe Weird Things*, wrote, "As it turns out, the accident rate is actually lower in the Bermuda Triangle than in surrounding areas."[27] The Cape of Good Hope off the southern tip of Africa and Cape Horn off the southern tip of South America are both watery graveyards far more fearsome than the Bermuda area. An area off the coast of Nova Scotia, Canada, is another spot that is more dangerous than the Bermuda area. Tens of thousands of lives have been lost in shipwrecks near a single island, Sable Island, off the coast of Nova Scotia. Many of these shipwrecks remain unexplained.

In the years since the publication of Kusche's book the tales of sudden vanishing airplanes and ships in the area known as the Bermuda Triangle have dried to a trickle. No updated best-sellers or documentaries alerting the public to the dangers have appeared. Hundreds of planes and ships pass safely through this area every day without incident or concern.

Yet the notion that a mysterious menace lurks in the Bermuda Triangle continues to flourish. The story of how that myth was created and continues to enjoy widespread belief today provides a fascinating lesson in human psychology.

Chapter 7

Why the Mystery Lingers

L ike most myths, the Bermuda Triangle legend sprouted from seeds of truth. There actually have been accidents and unexplained disappearances in the area. Veteran captains and pilots do not find such disappearances surprising. The ocean is a vast place subject to horrific, unpredictable storms. Airplanes and ships are imperfect machines, subject to mechanical and electrical failure. The people who operate them are fallible humans who make mistakes of observation and judgment. The combination of the three, say experts, is more than enough to explain a wide range of accidents and disappearances.

In the majority of the Bermuda Triangle mysteries that remain, the main cause of the puzzlement is not a set of supernatural or scientifically impossible events but simply a lack of information as to what happened. The disappearances of the *Mary Celeste* and the *Star Tiger* can never be explained because, unless some underwater explorer stumbles upon their remains, there is no way of obtaining further information about them.

However, some of the Bermuda Triangle stories, especially those from eyewitnesses who have survived harrowing encounters, report bizarre details that appear to be outside the normal laws of nature.

Heavy traffic

In addition, there have been a higher number of accidents in the Bermuda Triangle than in most other areas of the ocean. At first glance, this may sound like a contradiction of Kusche's findings, but it relates only to the number of accidents, not the rate at which accidents happen. The likelihood of an accident happening to any one plane or ship in the area is not high, but as Shermer points out, "Far more shipping lanes run through the Bermuda Triangle than its surrounding areas, so accidents and mishaps and disappearances are more likely to happen in the area."[28]

The U.S. Coast Guard's busiest base happens to be in Miami, where it handles more than eight thousand distress calls a year. According to the Coast Guard, this is not because of any exceptional hazards in the area but simply a result of sheer volume.

The Bermuda Triangle handles a large volume of shipping making the occurrence of mishaps more likely.

Contributing Bermuda Triangle Conditions

What made the area uniquely mysterious were the reports of ships, airplanes, and people that disappeared without a trace. There happen to be three physical features of the area that contributed to this absence of evidence.

One is the current. The Gulf Stream, one of the swiftest ocean currents in existence, runs directly through the Triangle. The force of this current can carry floating objects a great distance in a short time. That means that rescue ships and planes are not likely to find a downed plane, wrecked ship, survivors, or bodies near their last known location.

Another feature is the ocean depth. While parts of the Bermuda Triangle sea bottom lie within sight of the surface, the area also contains the Puerto Rico Trench, the deepest section of the Atlantic Ocean. Discovery of lost ships in this area, which plunges more than five miles below the ocean's surface, is next to impossible.

The crash of a Super Constellation cargo plane provided evidence of how quickly the seas in the Bermuda Triangle can swallow victims. On October 20, 1971, the plane, which was carrying a shipment of frozen sides of beef, suddenly plunged into the sea. The *R/V Discoverer* was in the vicinity and many of its crew saw exactly where the aircraft went down. The ship reached the crash site within fifteen minutes. As a research vessel, the *R/V Discoverer* was equipped with some of the most sophisticated detection gear in existence. Yet the crew found no trace of the wreckage except for a single side of beef. Not a sign of the aircraft, anyone on board, or even the tiniest oil slick ever turned up.

Finally, the area is subject to sudden, violent weather changes. An area that is reported as clear and sunny can be hit by a raging storm at a moment's notice. A sudden storm can blow damaged ships and planes far from their supposed

The weather within the Bermuda Triangle may change suddenly and unexpectedly.

locations. Unexpected high winds can also cause serious problems for an inexperienced navigator. A pilot unaware that he or she is flying into an eighty-mile-per-hour wind will be eighty miles short of the expected destination after an hour's flying time. Such winds will cause a pilot to report a faulty position to rescuers.

Need for Answers

Humans are uncomfortable with unsolved riddles. When answers are not readily available, people assemble the evidence as best they can and try to fashion educated guesses, plausible possibilities, and theories. According to experts on paranormal and other unexplainable events, coincidences create a special dilemma for curious humans.

Coincidences are events or circumstances that seem highly unlikely and yet occur anyway. Mathematically speaking, coincidences are inevitable, and many of them occur every day. If the odds against two-next door neighbors having the same first and last name are a million to one, then out of a sample of 10 million cases, the odds are that it will occur ten times.

The problem with coincidences, according to Michael Shermer, is that "we forget most of the insignificant coincidences and remember the meaningful ones."[29] In other words, when a particularly striking or bizarre coincidence appears, people take notice. They forget that coincidences occur all the time. They often search for the hidden reason or connection that causes the coincidence when, in fact, there is no connection other than they are the lottery winners in the law of averages.

According to scientific researchers, this tendency to search for hidden reasons or connections in striking coincidences lay at the root of the Bermuda Triangle myth. Coincidences occurred within a particular area in the form Five Avenger aircraft and a Martin Mariner all disappeared in the same evening. This happened near the same area where both the *Star Tiger* and *Star Ariel* vanished without a trace, and also happened to be in the same general vicinity as a number of sudden, major shipping disasters.

A poster about a missing yacht feeds the myth surrounding vessels lost in the Bermuda Triangle.

Researchers and amateur detectives spent a great deal of time and effort looking for the hidden reason behind the coincidences. As Kusche argued, it was a waste of time. He pointed out that many people die in traffic accidents under very similar circumstances—same speed, same weather conditions, same state of inebriation. Yet no one goes looking for some hidden force connecting all those deaths. Trying to find a common cause for the Bermuda Triangle disasters, he noted, makes no more sense than trying to find a common cause for those traffic accidents.

The urge to find hidden meaning in coincidence grows stronger when the coincidences occur far more frequently than the law of averages would predict. Vincent Gaddis originally was intrigued by some evidence that this was true of the Bermuda Triangle. Subsequent researchers, in pursuit of a fascinating story, then tended to focus only on reports and information that supported the belief that the Triangle was the home of an incredible number of strange occurrences. Researchers not only failed to check the truth of the Bermuda Triangle stories but withheld information, exaggerated, and distorted the truth.

Jumping to Conclusions

In an atmosphere of wild, terrifying claims, people tend to jump to conclusions, especially those conclusions that are consistent with their own pet theories about what is happening. English sailor Donald Crowhurst provides an example of how easily unexplained events and false conclusions can serve as fuel to feed the flames of distortion.

Crowhurst sailed from England on October 31, 1968, in his yacht, the *Teignmought Electron*, as the final contestant in a race sponsored by the *London Times*. The newspaper offered a large cash prize to the person who could sail around the world solo in the shortest amount of time. In June, Crowhurst was on the last leg of his long voyage. He reported his position as seven hundred miles southwest of the Azores. That was so far ahead of the pace of his nine rivals that Crowhurst appeared certain to claim the prize.

No one ever heard from Crowhurst again. On July 10, a British vessel spotted the *Teignmought Electron* drifting in the sea. On the verge of his hard-earned success, Crowhurst had vanished. The incident brought back eerie reminders of the *Mary Celeste* and others. In this case, though, Crowhurst left an explanation. The log book found on board described how he had plotted to win the prize by fraud. Instead of sailing around the world, he had spent the past six months circling the Atlantic and giving false reports of his position. As his moment of triumph neared, however, the man was overcome by shame. He stepped out of the boat into the sea and let the boat go on without him.

Crowhurst would have taken his place along with other prominent Bermuda Triangle victims, his fate subject to wild conjecture and pet theories, had he not left documentation of his actions and intentions.

Distrust of Authority

The Bermuda Triangle frenzy also fed on a widespread public distrust of authority. Even at the height of interest in the Bermuda Triangle, the U.S. Coast Guard steadfastly referred to it as "an imaginary area."[30] The U.S. Navy dismissed all reports of extraordinary danger in the triangle as fictitious. However, in an era when tales of government cover-ups were common, readers took seriously the statements of unidentified sources within the government who claimed the danger was real.

In such an environment, even innocent government testing became grist for rumors. When researchers discovered that the U.S. Navy was conducting magnetic tests in the Bermuda Triangle, they seized upon it as evidence of

The U.S. Navy has conducted geomagnetic surveys of all the earth's oceans including the area of the Bermuda Triangle.

the Navy's secret attempt to find the reason behind the frightening disappearances in the area. They failed to mention that the project did not target the Bermuda Triangle but involved airborne geomagnetic surveys of all the oceans.

Sensationalism Triumphs

The public's fascination with the bizarre and unexplained meant that the more sensational the version of events in the Bermuda Triangle, the more widespread attention that account received in the press. Even today, library shelves are crammed with books proclaiming paranormal powers, UFOs, and all sorts of mystical occurrences, while books debunking these claims are difficult to find.

In the case of the Bermuda Triangle, the media explosion over the sensational claims was exceptionally powerful and its effects long lasting. As an example, in May 1991 a salvage company headquartered in New York City cruised the ocean off the coast of Florida, searching for wrecks of Spanish galleons that had plundered the New World in the early colonial days. Using state-of-the-art sonar devices, Graham Hawkes and the crew of the Scientific Search Project found a cluster of five Navy Avenger torpedo-bombers within a 1.2-mile radius in 550 to 750 feet of water about ten miles off the coast of Fort Lauderdale, Florida. While most of the numbers were obscured, the aircraft were in good shape and the number "28" could been seen on one of the planes. That happened to be the number of Taylor's aircraft in Flight 19.

It appeared that the most famous victims of Bermuda Triangle, the Flight 19 Avengers, had shown up at last. Immediately the Bermuda Triangle stories which had lain dormant for many years resurfaced. Hawkes was swamped by reporters pursuing the Bermuda Triangle theme.

Upon closer inspection, Hawkes found that the tail numbers did not match those of the missing aircraft. Furthermore, the Avengers turned out to be model types older than those in Flight 19. The Navy explained that numbers of lost aircraft were often recycled and so "28" did not necessarily mean it was Taylor's plane.

The discovery of five lost Avengers in a cluster in the Bermuda Triangle, with one having the number 28, turned out to be nothing more than another bizarre coincidence. Ted Darcy, a marine archeologist noted that the Navy had used the area for many training missions during World War II. He calculated that at least 139 Avengers were lost off the coast of Florida. But the media furor over the incident showed that, despite Kusche's work, fascination with the diabolical legend was likely to remain for a long time.

Notes

Introduction

1. Quoted in Charles Berlitz, *The Bermuda Triangle*. New York: Avon, 1974, p. 42.
2. Berlitz, *The Bermuda Triangle*, p. 51.
3. Quoted in Adi-Kent Thomas Jeffrey, *The Bermuda Triangle*. New Hope, PA: New Hope Publications, 1973, p. 81.
4. Quoted in Al Snyder, *Satan's Sauna and the Devil's Triangle*. Redondo Beach, CA: Snyder Institute of Research, 1975, p. 18.

Chapter One: Ancient Fears and Legends of the Mid-Atlantic

5. Quoted in Jeffrey, *The Bermuda Triangle*, p. 9.
6. Jeffrey, *The Bermuda Triangle*, p. 9.
7. *Time*, "The Lost Squadron," May 27, 1991, p. 72.

Chapter Two: Ships Lost in the Triangle

8. Quoted in Martin Ebon, ed., *The Riddle of the Bermuda Triangle*. New York: New American Library, 1975, p. 64.

Chapter Three: Airplanes Lost in the Triangle

9. Quoted in Tom Post, "The Mystery of the Lost Patrol," *Newsweek*, May 27, 1991, p. 25.
10. John Wallace Spencer, *Limbo of the Lost*. New York: Bantam, 1974, p. 16.

11. Quoted in Berlitz, *The Bermuda Triangle*, p. 35.
12. Quoted in Berlitz, *The Bermuda Triangle*, p. 31.
13. Quoted in Post, "The Mystery of the Lost Patrol," p. 25.
14. Quoted in Berlitz, *The Bermuda Triangle*, p. 37.
15. Quoted in Spencer, *Limbo of the Lost*, p. 29.
16. Quoted in Spencer, *Limbo of the Lost*, p. 28.
17. Berlitz, *The Bermuda Triangle*, p. 45.

Chapter Four: Close Calls and Narrow Escapes

18. Quoted in Ebon, *The Riddle of the Bermuda Triangle*, p. 4.
19. Quoted in Richard Winer, *The Devil's Triangle*. New York: Bantam, 1977, p. 203.

Chapter Five: The Theories

20. Quoted in Richard Ellis, *Imagining Atlantis*, New York: Knopf, 1998, p. 51.
21. Spencer, *Limbo of the Lost*, p. 136.
22. Quoted in Jeffrey, *The Bermuda Triangle*, p. 78.

Chapter Six: The Rest of the Story

23. Quoted in Larry Kusche, *The Bermuda Triangle Mystery: Solved*, New York: Warner, 1975, p. 223.

24. Spencer, *Limbo of the Lost*, p. 4.

25. Quoted in Kusche, *The Bermuda Triangle Mystery*, p. 114.

26. Quoted in Winer, *The Devil's Triangle*, p. 13.

27. Michael Shermer, *Why People Believe Weird Things*. New York: W. H. Freeman, 1997, p. 55.

Chapter Seven: Why the Mystery Lingers

28. Shermer, *Why People Believe Weird Things*, p. 55.

29. Shermer, *Why People Believe Weird Things*, p. 54.

30. Quoted in Ebon, *The Riddle of the Bermuda Triangle*, p. 124.

For Further Reading

Charles Berlitz, *The Bermuda Triangle*. New York: Avon, 1974. This readable presentation is representative of the flurry of books that came out in the early 1970s supporting the existence of the Bermuda Triangle.

Larry Kusche, *The Bermuda Triangle Mystery: Solved*. New York: Warner, 1975. This is the book that carefully and thoroughly punctured the Bermuda Triangle myths. Although not aimed at juvenile readers, the reading is not difficult.

Works Consulted

Books

George O. Abell and Barry Singer, eds., *Science and the Paranormal*. New York: Charles Scribner's Sons, 1983. A compilation of viewpoints discussing the validity of paranormal claims.

Martin Ebon, ed., *The Riddle of the Bermuda Triangle*. New York: New American Library, 1975. A collection of articles from writers with a wide variety of viewpoints on the subject, including Vincent Gaddis and Larry Kusche.

Richard Ellis, *Imagining Atlantis*. New York: Knopf, 1998. This straightforward book debunks claims of the lost continent.

Adi-Kent Thomas Jeffrey, *The Bermuda Triangle*. New Hope, PA: New Hope Publications, 1973. This is an undocumented account of the Bermuda Triangle legend from a believer's viewpoint.

Michael Shermer, *Why People Believe Weird Things*. New York: W. H. Freeman, 1997. This is an interesting examination of the reasons why incredible claims are often more popular than scientific proofs.

Al Snyder, *Satan's Sauna and the Devil's Triangle*. Redondo Beach, CA: Snyder Institute of Research, 1975. This is another legend account of the Bermuda Triangle.

John Wallace Spencer, *Limbo of the Lost*. New York: Bantam, 1974. This legend account is from the perspective of a former pilot who believes UFOs are responsible for the disappearances in the Bermuda Triangle.

Richard Winer, *The Devil's Triangle*. New York: Bantam, 1977. The last popular book to come out on the Bermuda Triangle, it puts forth subdued claims in the light of Kusche's exposé.

Periodicals

Tim Golden, "Mystery of Bermuda Triangle Remains One," *New York Times*, June 5, 1991.

National Geographic World, "The Bermuda Triangle," December 1989.

Tom Post, "The Mystery of the Lost Patrol," *Newsweek*, May 27, 1991.

Time, "The Lost Squadron," May 27, 1991.

Index

Picture Credits

About the Author

Nathan Aaseng is the author of more than 150 books for young readers on a wide variety of subjects. Aaseng, from Eau Claire, Wisconsin, was a 1999 recipient of the Wisconsin Library Association's Notable Wisconsin Author award.